THE BOSUN CHAIR

JENNIFER BOWERING DELISLE

THE BOSUN CHAIR

Library and Archives Canada Cataloguing in Publication

Delisle, Jennifer, 1979-, author
The bosun chair / Jennifer Bowering Delisle.

Based on the author's thesis submitted to the University of Alberta 2003.
Issued in print and electronic formats.
ISBN 978-1-926455-87-7 (paperback).--ISBN 978-1-926455-88-4 (epub).--ISBN 978-1-926455-89-1 (mobi)

1. Newfoundland and Labrador--Poetry. I. Title.

PS8607.E4844B67 2017 C811'.6 C2016-905877-8
C2016-905878-6

Board Editor: Jenna Butler
Cover design & layout: Kate Hargreaves
Author photograph: Jennifer Bowering Delisle
Interior photographs care of Jennifer Bowering Delisle
Cover photograph: Tim Boote

Canada Council for the Arts Conseil des Arts du Canada
Funded by the Government of Canada
Financé par le gouvernement du Canada
Canada

access© Alberta Government The City of Edmonton edmonton arts council

NeWest Press acknowledges the support of the Canada Council for the Arts, the Alberta Foundation for the Arts, and the Edmonton Arts Council for support of our publishing program. This project is funded in part by the Government of Canada.

NeWest Press
201, 8540 – 109 Street
Edmonton, AB T6G 1E6
780.432.9427
www.newestpress.com

No bison were harmed in the making of this book.

PRINTED AND BOUND IN CANADA

1 2 3 4 5 19 18 17

For Malcolm and Coralie, so you may build your own histories.

CONTENTS

PROLOGUE

IN JUNE OF 1915, LIKE EVERY JUNE, Captain John Bowering of Coley's Point, Newfoundland, set sail on the *Swallow* for the season's fishing in Labrador. By the time he and his crew were ready to return home at the end of October, the ship was so full of fish that some of the sailors were left behind to return on the *Lorna Doone.*

Mid dangers thick, seen and unseen,
On waves which smash our barque,—
A sailor's life is hard indeed;
And oft' the way seems dark.

His ballad "Trip of the Ill-Fated *Swallow*" was printed by someone in the family in little twenty-page booklets, covered in red card stock. In the tiny type he tells me, his great-granddaughter, the story in quaint rhyme.

Now all on board, — ready to sail,
That fine October day;

All hoped a breeze of North West wind,
Would hurry us on our way.

My parents left Newfoundland when they were twenty-three. They were not fishers pushed by empty nets, outport people in search of black prairie gold. But Alberta called them nevertheless, with a residency at the U of A Hospital for Dad and a whole province pulsing with oil money. Four thousand people a month came in those days. My parents did not plan to stay in Edmonton. They have never left.

My parents had aunts and uncles who moved to Calgary and Vancouver in the '40s. A brother already in Winnipeg. More of the family would follow them, to Grande Prairie, Fort St. John, Houston. The population of the province is only half a million, and they say that more than 200,000 Newfoundlanders live "away." But that 200,000 does not include the children of Newfoundlanders born in Toronto, or Boston, or Fort McMurray. I am one of that unknown number who grew up hearing Newfoundland called "home."

Jean Chaulk was just sixteen when she set sail aboard the merchant schooner *The Duchess of Fife* in September of 1907. A maid working in St. John's, catching a ride home to her family, she may have been the only passenger, a favour from her cousin on the crew.

We left St. John's on Monday morn,
Our spirits were light and gay.
We were bound home to Brookland,
In Bonavista Bay.

Her poem "The Loss of the *Duchess of Fife*" is typed on plain legal paper, photocopied many times and curling at the edges. I don't know who typed the poem, or when.

While Carbonear we reached that night,
And early left next morn,
To run for Catalina,
As our captain feared the storm.

It must mean something that my great-grandparents on either side of my family wrote poems. It must mean that despite a distance of a hundred years and three thousand miles, there is a connection between us that runs deeper than the DNA. A line that I can follow back across a continent.

When I was growing up, I was angry with my parents for leaving Newfoundland. I wrote sentimental stories and poems set there, describing the pattern of tide against the rocky shore or the smell of salt in the air. On visits from St. John's, my grandfather told tales of a conspiracy behind Confederation, how St. John's was draped in black on the day Newfoundland joined Canada. We were taught in school that Canada is a mosaic. My friends were Ukrainian, Indian, Chinese—we were all born in Edmonton. My heritage was Newfoundland. This was where I looked for rootedness, a kind of belonging.

Make no wonder, my mother might say.

Make no wonder. I was a grown woman before I knew that that was a Newfoundlandism, adding on the "make" to that certain phrase.

While here upon the trackless deep,
So far away from home;
The thought comes forcibly to my mind,
We know not where we'll roam.

As the *Swallow* was heading toward home, the weather turned. A gale charged in, the seas began to pummel her sides. One by one the sails burst under the hurricane winds. The heavy sea swept the wheel aside and the foremast threatened to topple.

As *The Duchess of Fife* approached the harbour at Catalina, the storm the captain had feared surrounded her, wrenching away the main boom, leaving the schooner to drift all night in the taunting swells.

Both ships were left to the mercy of the wind.

THREE THOUSAND QUINTALS

IT WAS A GIANT DOLL'S HOUSE, without a back wall. I wanted to follow my father as he picked through the rotten boards, the cobwebs, the barrels of china whose plates, held up to the light, shone clean through the dark room. But Mom held my hand.

My grandfather was a wooden boy, donning old-fashioned clothes by the crackle of the fire. My great-grandfather was made of paper, eating fish and brewis at the table before running off to school.

I thought we could take the china, but we left it there. It doesn't belong to us, Dad said. Meaning there were uncles and aunts who also belonged to this place, who grew up and moved away, whose lives here were not pretend, just long ago.

From my spot in the yard, the old room was the size of my small palm.

Someone humming that old song "She's Like the Swallow" as he loads the barrels of salt, the crates of tea and hard tack, into the holds for the long northern summer.

She's like the swallow that flies so high…
I love my love and love is no more.

The Swallow, Fradsham's two-masted schooner. Someone named her this, thinking of a white flapping: the mainsail and topsail, the flying jib. Or thinking of Sir Humphrey's old ship, alongside *The Squirrel* and *The Golden Hind,* in which he claimed the New Founde Land for England—back when a bucket, they say, could be lowered in the water and come up again full of fish. Forgetting the tragic Newfoundland song, the maiden scorned by her lover who lays down to die—

She took her roses and made a bed, a stony pillow for her head.

Thinking instead of the long migration to the Labrador, the flocks that fished for cod in the Strait of Belle Isle, as far as Cape Chidley, the northern tip of coast that looks across the Hudson Strait to Baffin Island.

She's like the sunshine on the lee shore…
She's lost her love and she'll love no more.

But swallows at sea are a good omen, so long as no one whistles on board, or coils a rope against the sun.

The schooner loaded, the weather fine, Captain John Bowering kisses his wife Rhoda and daughter Nellie on the beach. Sixty people board with him for the ten-day journey to the fish.

Coley's Point began as Cold East Point, a good beach in Conception Bay for the fishermen of Jersey to dry their catch. Became the warm cove of some imagined man named Coley, who still searches the coastline for the point to lead him home.

Conception Bay, once the fishery's fecund source; in 1915 it is already scraped raw. Half the men of Coley's Point venture north to the Labrador for a summer at the fish. Then south for a winter in the coal mines of Sydney, then north again for a spring on the ice when the seals perch on pans heaving on the ocean.

A summer on the Labrador: four-thousand-foot fjords flanked by icebergs and tiny islands, guiding the schooners to their rooms. They call them rooms, the little fishing stations where the fish are made, as though these ramshackle stores were a house, as though this cold bit of coast were home.

A quick mug-up of hard bread and tea and the men crack their morning joints towards the cod traps. Balanced in their skiffs, they heave the nets out of the water, hoping for the ache of a heavy haul breaking the surface. By 7:30 a.m. the first loads have already been pitchforked onto the stagehead.

Put away the fish: simple as plates in a cupboard, clean as socks in a drawer. The cutthroat slits the fish with a double-bladed knife. The header lops the head and entrails, and the splitter, the skipper, slips out the backbone before the salter puts the fish in the salt barrels.

Make the fish: simple as tea, clean as bread. Wash the salted fish, then pile them for the night—piles six feet wide, drained by the weight of their own flesh. Spread them on the flakes to dry for the day in the sun and the flies, pile them up again at night, spread them again, pile them up, covered in spruce boughs, covered in flies. Watch for dryness and signs of sunburn, watch for bad weather. Spread them out again, until the fish is dry and hard.

By October, the work is done. More than 3,000 quintals of fish. Not as good as they'd hoped, but it should bring in enough for winter.

Behind the house, from tiny eyes closed with earth, the potatoes grow in rows. Rhoda picks out the weeds and rocks around them, leaning up the slope, her back to the water.

These things were planted before he left, and now are pushing upward, skinned with dirt. The potatoes and the carrots will be barrelled and sold, save the ones cellared for the winter. The best heads of cabbage will be pickled in salt, like round green fish.

The sun is warm for fall as she lifts her skirts out of the dirt, and when she closes her eyes she can see her own blood through her most fragile skin. She has buried other things too in this ground, things that will not grow.

Soon it will be time to harvest the potatoes, and if he has not returned, she will dig them up alone.

So much fish was loaded on to the *Swallow* that forty-three people returned to Bay Roberts on the *Lorna Doone.* Seventeen went on the *Swallow.*

That night the wind was good and free,
A breeze of North West wind;
We glided up the shore, and left
Old Domino behind.

The crew: Samuel Kinsella, William Russell, Arthur Greenland, and the cook Clara King of Country Road. Ten freighters—passengers returning from a season's work at the fish—John Jones of Upper Island Cove, three Battens of Bareneed, and others from Clarke's Beach. Skipper John Bowering of Coley's Point, and 1,400 quintals of fish.

Had the wind held another twenty-four hours, they would have been home. Instead, the *Swallow* floated through St. Anthony, Englee, White Bay, Green Bay, slow as a dory. In her lee, the storm-petrels followed low to the water, picking at the plankton churned in her wake. For two weeks she waited for the wind in Seldom-Come-By, as if to console the village for its lonely name.

When the wind finally came, it came determined to make up for lost time, blowing away their own breath, making them gasp like fish on the stagehead. They reefed the sails, tried to get the foresail down as it began to tear. Cabot Island was ahead. They tacked the schooner and managed to get around the island, the jumbo and the jib tearing behind them.

We lowered our mainsail—all seemed dark,
Crushed, hopes of getting home;
We ran her then before the wind;
We knew not what would come.

This is what comes: the foresail bursts the rigging. A cask of cod oil knocks the wheel out of place. The foresail blows away. The mast heaves open the deck like the key on a can. The sea sweeps over, smashing a small boat on deck, hurling molasses puncheons over the rail. The ship's constant roll bursts the tackles rigged to hold the mast in place.

This is what comes: a storm that does not relent for days, stripping the schooner of her canvas, prying apart the fingers of the planks that grip them above the waves.

Before it is tucked between the logs of the stove, she peeks at the pages of the *Bay Roberts Guardian,* reading as the bread is rising.

> The body of John B. Mercer was the only one recovered among the 23 Nfld. Reservists lost on the H.M.S. Viknor.
>
> The death of Mrs. Flight, who resided at Chelsea, Mass., occurred at that place sometime ago. Mrs. Flight was formerly Miss Bertha Russell, of Country Road.

Formerly, she thinks, no longer a Russell, neither a Flight any longer.

> Deceased was afflicted with the dread disease consumption, and knowing there was no hope for her, she longed for the end to come.
>
> Hun Shipping has Suffered Heavily.
>
> ARCTIC INDIGESTION CURE! CAN YOU DOUBT THESE WORDS? I WAS A SUFFERER FOR 18 YEARS!

All this death, all this useless news. She pokes the paper into the pyre and lights it, bringing the cold stove to life to make her bread.

John tried to lighten her by throwing their summer's work, the fish, overboard. The ship was turning to water. Her deck was a landwash flooded with waves, her hull was sand washing out from beneath their feet. They pumped for their lives, without pausing to wipe the salt from their eyes. But John knew that the *Swallow* would never make it back to land.

In a few days, the petrels, too, would wreck on the beaches, exhausted from fighting the winds, starved of plankton on the turbulent sea.

On the fourth night, just after dark, the distant light of a steamer heading west. They paused in their pumping, lighting desperate flares, blowing their horn, praying that the steamer would turn. But the ship continued on her course and disappeared.

By October she begins to watch the horizon, as if to spot him as he crests the hill. She could see him now but for the fog. A broad smile as he scoops up his daughter and tells of his record catch. Then leaning into tales of his summer.

Other schooners begin to return, the *Jennie Jones,* the *Hope.* The *Lorna Doone* makes it back to Bay Roberts with the bulk of the crew, but by November there is still no sign of the *Swallow*. Finally, a one-line wire from Seldom to the company to say that they are on their way, and then the storm devours the coast, and the *Swallow* vanishes.

The storm brought down telegraph lines all over—they may be safe and just unable to wire. He's having tea in Catalina this afternoon. He's setting out from Bay de Verde now and heading home.

As November wears on, other schooners caught in the storm stumble into ports. The *Florence* had safely run for Portugal Cove, and then was towed back to Bay Roberts by the Bell Island steamer. The *Rattler* made it in to Little Catalina; the crew of the *Blanche M. Rose* were rescued from their wreck by the *May Duff* and taken to Sydney. And still no sign of the *Swallow*.

The ship was filling with water like a dipping spoon. It was the fifth night since the storm began, and they began to lose hope.

But no! The scene did quickly change;
For at ten o'clock that night,
While anxious eyes were looking hard,
One shouted "There's a light."

They fired muskets and flares made with oil clothes and twine soaked in cod oil, until the steamer's light changed shape, became two across the night. Port and starboard. It was changing course. It was coming their way.

As the lifeboats rowed toward the steamer, John looked back at the ship they had abandoned. For nearly a week they had fought day and night to keep the schooner above water. He had begun to get used to the idea of being the captain who goes down with the ship.

Aboard the steamer, he discovered that she was a Norwegian ship called the *Hercules*. They had drifted many miles, and the *Hercules* was bound for Europe.

Rhoda sits with her mother-in-law knitting in dim lantern light, purling tea and wood smoke into the yarn. For the old lady, the needles' rhythmic clicking is comforting, meditative. For Rhoda, it is a clock, tapping out the time that is gone.

Mother knits little mittens for her granddaughter, the white wool jigging against her knee. Rhoda knits a new pair of stockings for her husband's next season on the Labrador. If he is dead, she is wasting time that should be spent on cleaning the stove, on polishing the tea stains from the cups. If he is alive, then he will need his stockings, perhaps even a new sweater, underwear, and other things for the spring. This unrelenting rhythm, *purl purl purl, knit knit knit.*

TO: The Captain, Mates, Engineers and other members of the crew of S.S. Hercules

We the undersigned do hereby wish to express our thanks and gratitude to you for your kindness and hospitality shown to us in our distress. I am sure words fail to express how we feel toward you when we think of how you have rescued us from the sinking schooner.

The kind actions you have done for us; the kind words you have spoken to us as strangers during our stay with you shall not soon be erased from our memory. And wherever it may be our lot to go and whenever we may look upon a Norwegian Captain or sailor we shall always look upon him as a friend and in our hearts shall be found a warm place for him.

As we have nothing financially to compensate you, we trust that our superiors and those who represent us and our country shall not fail to amply reward you and I know the great God of the universe, who has not failed to see your actions, shall much more reward you.

I trust it will not be your lot to pass through such an ordeal as we have passed but, if it may, I trust you may find in an Englishman or some other nationality such a friend as we have found in you. May I say in conclusion, I trust that you will arrive safely home in due time and that you may be prospered on whatever voyage you may go.

Signed
Captain and Crew of Swallow
Nov. 30th, 1915

BAY ROBERTS GUARDIAN, FRIDAY, NOV 26, 1915

SCHR. SWALLOW STILL UNREPORTED

The schr Swallow, John Bowering, master, and owned by Fradsham & Co., bound from Domino to Bay Roberts with freighters and a load of fish, is still unreported. The vessel left Seldom Come By with other schooners on Monday and was caught in the terrific storm of Tuesday, Nov, 16th.

The friends of those on board have been very anxious regarding the fate of their loved ones, and early in the week sent messages to the Marine and Fisheries Dept. requesting that a steamer be sent to search for the vessel.

They learned that on Friday the steamers Ingraham and Cabot were sent out, but they cruised chiefly in a southerly direction. The Cabot took the rescued crew of the little schr. Annie from another steamer which rescued them and brought them into Fermeuse.

Both steamers returned to St John's on Wednesday, having seen nothing of the other missing vessels. Steps should in our opinion and in the opinion of others, have been taken earlier in the week to have a search made and the largest and fastest steamers available should have been sent out. Three or four days passed away before a search was commenced.

The Cabot left again Thursday night to continue the search for the Swallow. It is very probable that the Swallow drifted south in the way of shipping and that those on board have been rescued before this.

She wants to believe, when his sister bursts breathless into the kitchen, a fluttering gull above the stage, that what she says is true: that the fortune teller she saw knows that he is safe. She wants to believe that he will return on Christmas Day, as foretold in the lines of leaves or palms, that this is not pagan nonsense, but a small new Christmas miracle. She wants to believe, even as she tells her, his sister, that she is dull to believe in such things, even as she feels her small bones crush beneath the words on her teeth.

Rumours that the ship has been spotted on Locker Flat Island in Bonavista Bay, a three-mile-long island with shores of shelving rock beneath the water. The Minister of Marine and Fisheries has sent a motor boat to search for the ship among the islands of Locker Reach.

She heats a beach rock in the stove, wraps it in a towel and brings it to bed. It weighs down the mattress, just a little, on his side, where his elbow would nestle into her chest. How many quintals? Are you eating enough? How is Clara King's cooking? Let me tend your hands, I'll dress the salt water boils on your knuckles with a cool bread poultice, while I tell you about the new baby that Mrs. Russell had, the snow that fell this afternoon. Nellie said a new word today. Her voice comes some soft and small from her tiny mouth, and sometimes I want to swallow her, safe back into my body. *Soup*, she said. I made pea soup today with you in my mind, thick with fatty pork so that the spoon would barely sink. Let me heat you some, that'll warm you, it must be cold on the water tonight. 'Tis a cold night. Before she is asleep the rock is cool.

Eight days at sea, getting used to the new sound of the ship's steel belly. Drawing nearer to a war that had been as far from Labrador as the bottom of the ocean from the light. They hadn't known that soldiers spent the summer locked in French mud, that the Germans had captured Warsaw in August, that the Newfoundland Regiment was in the Dardanelles. Drawing into the trenches of the Atlantic's waves, where submarines sharked unseen.

They were stopped by a British cruiser that checked their papers and escorted them to Stornoway, a small Gaelic port town on the Isle of Lewis. They were citizens of the British Empire, but Norway was neutral, and in letters spies had written the location of British ships in invisible ink. The Custom House officer told him he wasn't supposed to send them home.

I said "That thing seemed awful strange,
And hard to understand;
Norwegian sailors were so good,
As to bring us in to land.

And here among our British friends,
There's nothing can be done;
And is it possible you say
We cannot be sent home."

His speech did not rhyme. Between these lines, quiet as ink on paper, is a hidden rhythm, the timbre of a man two thousand miles from home, who negotiates with waves, not men. Was he the sort of man who made demands or made friends? Had the storm's surges hewn him like a beach stone, or like a knife? Did he gently remove the backbone of his words? Did he plead, did he slam a fist on the table?

The officer sent a message to Liverpool stating their case to the Board of Trade, and the next day made arrangements for them to go to Liverpool in two days time. They left at 4 a.m. on a steamer to Kyle, where they would leave the sea and continue their journey by train. It was the beginning of December.

When daylight came, and we could see
Along the Scottish shore;
The hills were covered in with snow,
Almost like Labrador.

These lamplight stanzas roll,
seabirds riding the windshear,
groundfish on deep currents.

Does he imagine me,
eating these hard-fought verses
pulled from the deep pressure of the ocean
its pinching fickleness?
Will he set them before his children
carefully removing the tiniest of bones?

The iamb mouths at the story
and the rhyme hangs on the line,
like drops of cold water.

Someone is running. From the Bay Roberts cable building, down Water Street, across the Klondyke Bridge. The old folks here remember dumping the rock and gravel into the open water gashed in the ice, to build the causeway. Their fathers and mothers had carried the rock in hand-barrels and the children had piled stones in their arms, for the goldrush wage of a dollar a week. Now ice again fills the coish, and ice shines the boy's steps into Coley's Point, along the road to the Bowering house. In the pocket of his coat crinkles the paper of a telegram, a message that came across the ocean in dots like scattered stones.

London, Dec 1st
To Governor:
Following for Minister of Marine and Fisheries from master of Swallow: Crew and passengers saved and landed, all well, at Stornoway, on Norwegian steamer Herkules. Please circulate information.
(Sgd,) John Bowering

We are alive.
We are coming home.

From Kyle, a train for Inverness, then another for Perth, then another for Wigham, then another for Liverpool, finally stumbling from the train at 6 a.m., feeling its rumble still in their bones the way they always felt the sea floating their feet after stepping on dry land.

In Bay Roberts, the first electric lights had been turned on last spring, lighting the railway station, two streetlights and the telegraph house. Liverpool was dawn before the morning, streetlights spotlighting the grey snow, a city throbbing with motor cars and tram cars flushed with immigrants.

They had to get a passport to prove they were British citizens before they would be allowed on a ship, dogged by questions from the Board of Trade. Then a week waiting for the *Pretorian* to sail for Canada.

On December tenth, they were at sea again. At night, all the lights were out on deck for fear of German submarines. The seas were rolling high, familiar as the stink of their own bodies after a day at the fish. They stayed below, sick in their beds, waiting for the rogue wave across the deck, or the final white shock of a torpedo. Eleven days and nights in darkness and heavy seas until they finally docked in Saint John, New Brunswick.

It took several hours for all hands to pass the emigration officer, and they could not arrange to leave Saint John until that night. Two more days by train and ship to get to Port aux Basques on the west coast of Newfoundland. But the train was four hours late; they missed their connection and had to wait for the night train at Brigus Junction. They finally arrived in Bay Roberts on Christmas Day, two months after they had started for home, six months since they had last seen their families.

BAY ROBERTS GUARDIAN, FRIDAY, DEC 31, 1915

THE SWALLOW'S SURVIVORS RETURN HOME

Details of Their Hard Experience

The crew and passengers of the ill-fated schr. Swallow reached their various homes on Saturday (Christmas) night, Dec. 25th. At Clarke's Beach and Bay Roberts stations hundreds of people gathered to extend to them a glad welcome, and this was proof of the deep interest which was manifested in their rescue and their return to home and loved ones.

With the limited time at our disposal this week we have managed to glean the following particulars regarding the trip of the Swallow and the awful time experienced by those on board during the storm which commenced on Tuesday, Nov. 26th, up to the time of their rescue and of their arrival home.

...The mast was rocking to and fro and the deck was opening fast. After sometime a brace was placed against the spar. Three days passed and still the storm continued. The main rigging then burst and the deck was torn open. The vessel began to leak and things looked very gloomy for those on board.

One pump alone was kept going the second one being useless, while a good watch was kept for any passing ship. A quantity of fish was thrown overboard to lighten the vessel. The girls on board kept up a good heart and encouraged the men...

BAY ROBERTS GUARDIAN, JAN 14, 1916.

THE TRIP OF THE "SWALLOW"

(Editor the Guardian).

Dear Sir, -- As there has been a lot of strange statements rumored, and also a note or two which appeared in last week's issue concerning our hard experience seemed so ridiculous, I feel prompted to give you my statement so near to the thing as I can go.

On the 15th day of November, about 7 p.m., we left Seldom-Come-Bye bound for Bay Roberts. The wind was blowing a fresh breeze from the north-west, and all hoped that within the next 24 hours we would reach our destination.

The poem says nothing of his wife's worry through his absence, nothing of how the families made it through winter with no fish to bring home and a debt to the merchant that could not be paid. He cannot write how once he returned, he never went to sea again, but became a carpenter, made barrels for potatoes and fish. Had seven more children, four of whom died before the age of eighteen.

...All this happened at about the one time—the foresail jibed, the casks broke loose, the wheel was knocked out of its place and the boat was smashed up. This made things look quite gloomy...

We sawed off the jaws of a main boom we had lashed on deck and put it down around the foot of the mast and let the end go against the side of the vessel. We also tried to secure the rigging by putting tackles on the ends of the shrouds and strops around the bulwarks; but with such a heavy sway it was impossible to secure it good.

He supported his family building houses in Grand Falls and St. John's, and still found himself far away from his family for months at a time.

...On the evening of the 10th we left Liverpool by the S.S. Pretorian of the Allan Line for St. John, N.B., arriving at the latter place on Dec. 21st, where the Shipping Master gave us a railway pass to Bay Roberts via North Sydney and Port au Basques, arriving at Bay Roberts on the 25th (Christmas Day) a long round indeed from Domino.

With all sympathy for the girls in passing through such an ordeal I must say that note in the last issue has put the few brave fellows who stood by me and worked so faithfully in the face of such dangers down in a very low place, to say they had to be encouraged by a few girls. Yours, etc.

JOHN BOWERING

The next time I returned, the house was completely gone. Grass had grown over the stumps of walls, thistle cluttered the rooms. Embedded in the ground was half a teacup stained with soil. Surely she had lifted it to her mouth, waiting for her husband to return, to stomp the snow from his boots and lay them by the stove. The fragments interrupted the weeds, like stories buried in the earth: She puts her knitting down, pulls him in, kisses him with tea-warm lips.

BALLYCATER

HAVE YOU EVER HEARD OF BALLYCATER? Ballycater, there must be a more scientific name for it but as far as I know it's B-A-L-L-Y-C-A-T-E-R, it's ballycater. You might find another word in a dictionary or some book, but it was big pans of ice. And sometimes they would fill up the harbour. And we would go down, and hop from one pan to the next, and as you stepped on the pans they had a tendency to go under. And then of course there were several coming behind you, everybody's stepping on the pans, and you had to try to get from one pan to the next without getting your feet wet. And also hoping that the next pan wouldn't be too far away so you could hop to it.

They called it copying, this game. They copied their fathers heading out on the ice for the seals, just as they had copied their mothers, feeding dolls with spoons of grass. My grandmother is copying on the ballycater, the pans tipping dangerously as she lands near the edge. Leaning forward, pantsuit and nylon stockings, grey hair dyed pale blonde, icy water flooding pink slippers.

My father used to leave to go to the Labrador in May and he wouldn't return home until September? October? And I can remember stormy nights saying to Mom, "My gosh, I wonder how's Dad." And that's when it would come in my mind, mostly when we had storms. And then she used to say "Oh, don't worry, because this is only here where we are. They're not having any storms where he is, that's too far away."

Pop was a winter father. She did not know him in shirt sleeves on the beach, or in the garden. He came like Father Christmas with the cold, his sweater smelling of fish and wool wet with the first snow.

And maybe that was true, but of course they're having storms down there when we don't know about it. But because there was no way we could contact them we didn't know where they were, or how they were, or anything until they got home. She was pretty optimistic and accepted that as a way of life, really. They were worried, you know they were worried but that was a part of life, that's the way of life in Newfoundland.

We used to go to a place called Shepherd's Pond, which is known for its abundance of trout, fishing through the ice, you know. And on a nice day like today now, when the sun was shining and a good sleigh path, my father always used to say to Mom "Now today would be a nice day to go into Shepherd's Pond, see if we can get a trout."

On the tape, the crackle of tin foil as my mother makes dinner. Atlantic salmon farmed on the west coast, bought from an Edmonton Costco. I strain to catch the words—rewind, stop, play again. Dog sleigh full of trout and the day dimming to the light off the snow. Streaks of black where they know the woods are, black where they know the sky is. Then black where the ice is, where the ice should be on the path ahead, where the water has shed its icy skin.

My mother told me this story, they were in Shepherd's Pond trouting and it was getting dark.

Stories too slippery to steady on. The oven door opens, the television news. And the dogs are heading for the water, and the dogs are going too fast to stop them. And Pop is pushing Nan off the sleigh, and jumping after her, and the dogs go on, into the water.

In that black cleft are the questions I did not ask: if she was in school or if this was before she was born, if they saved the dogs, how they got home without the sleigh. Stop, rewind.

I can hear my father say to my mother now, "This'll be a nice day to go to Shepherd's Pond."

Pop called his schooner the *Ivy Frances* for his youngest, and so took his girls with him like a photograph in his pocket. In Little Heart's Ease he was the privileged one, the Skipper, the one who owned the store and the post office, whose wealth was measured by his debt.

Credit from the merchant in St. John's for the ropes and the nets, for the oilskins and boots for the twelve men on the schooner, for the food that stocked the ship and the food that stocked the store to feed the families of the men for the summer. Credit to the men for their oilskins and boots, for the flour that sustained their children while their fathers were away. There had to be fish. There had to be enough for the men to pay him their debts, so that he could pay his own in St. John's, when the winter came and the last of the fall's carrots were gnarled in the bottom of the bin like beckoning fingers. There had to be fish.

She fished from the wharf, where she and her sister would line up the connors and play at grief, pretending they had a cemetery. Where they screamed and dropped their rods when they pulled a sculpin grunting from the water, the monsters with their jurassic teeth and spines. Where the water was deep enough for the schooners to unload, and the logs were iced with seaweed, and the children didn't know how to swim. *And we went for help, calling out to someone to come—Donny, his name was Donny, I'll never forget his name was Donny, "Donny's in the water! Donny's in the water!"* And the memory of the men plucking Donny from the water, barely breathing but alive, makes her think not of her own small feet balanced on the edge of the wharf greased with fish, but of her mother, watching from a window or the road, watching the bodies of her daughters small and slippery at the water's edge.

To make fish n' brewis, soak the hard tack and the salt fish overnight. Then, when you can see the team of dogs coming over the hill with the firewood, put the bread and the fish on to boil. Serve them together with pork scruncheons or drawn butter.

If you are on a ship, bags of hard tack will last months without going mouldy. And if you are on land and too poor to eat the fish that your father caught last summer, the stones of hard tack will soften slowly in the hollow of your cheek.

I was very young but I can remember people coming in the shop to get what they called a dole note filled? I can see those notes now. It was written on it flour, sugar, butter, the bare necessities for food, you know.

And the relieving officer was such that he got his job because he was such a hard man—that's what they say, and I believe it, too. I know people who have walked from a place called St. Joseph's, right up to the country—oh, it must be about what, God, maybe twelve miles to walk, in the winter time up to his office—and he would say, "Now see here, in the last six months you had so many weeks work. No. I can't give you a dole note." And that man would have to turn around and walk back again, those long long distances, with nothing. No note.

No dust bowls in this Depression, no parched prairie cracked open with drought. Here there was water for miles, and there was work. They worked to pay for their nets and boots, for the food they gave their children, the hard bread they gnawed till their jaws were sore. They fished for fish that did not belong to them, in a place where you could starve by an ocean still full of cod. A Depression you could drown in.

You know if my father had a dollar, he would give half of it away, you know? He couldn't stand to see someone suffering if he had anything to give him. And he gave away more than one pan of flour to people who didn't have any flour to make bread. He said, "I never want for anything, no. I never want for it. I've got enough to do me."

When he returns from the Labrador the relief of home is clot with thoughts about the catch and its worth, the merchants in the city and the rating their cullers will give each fish.

Merchantable, that's what you're after. Madeira—less than eighteen inches. West Indies, the cullage—sunburned, saltburned, blood spots. Poor fish for the poor of Barbados, and a poor price for the poor of Newfoundland.

Each fish they have handled fifty times, catching, splitting, washing, salting, spreading; the fish were shielded from weather, swaddled in rinds, touched more than their wives.

The culler paws at the stacks, hurling yaffles of good fish into the cullage and Pop stands silent, surrounded by men, hundreds of men waiting for their turn with their schooners cradling their own fish, watching as the culler, that stunned arse ugly as a sculpin cocks his head like he's done him a favour and reduces his year's work to a note of debt.

And I remember saying to him one time, "Oh I wish you wouldn't go to Labrador anymore, why can't you stay home now." And I remember him saying to me, "Well maybe another year or so and I won't have to go to Labrador and I'll be able to stay home." But that last time he was down, I heard him say about so many thousand dollars in debt, didn't make any money. No fish. And that was when he decided to sell the schooner.

She leaves this place to teach school in other towns on the coast. She worries for her pupils balanced on the ice pans. She knows the pull of the ice, gathered along the shore. She, too, was once immortal.

In choosing names for her own she will think of these children, the students who were too raucous, or slow. She will hope for a girl and get four boys. She will catch them on the counters, pretending the floor is lava, and envision cracked skulls and broken necks.

Ice is building now on the eaves. I know her alone with a burnt porch light. I know her pointing to a wharf taken long ago by the ice. They say I look like her, in black and white youth, before grief caught her, ignoring her talisman of worry.

That way is the depths of the North Atlantic. That way, too, is home. The ballycater sits in the cove like a hundred white rafts. Hold your coat closed at the neck and follow the path down to the water.

On a clear evening she walked with her sweetheart back from Ganny Cove up the arm, their toes growing numb in their boots and their hands warmed in each other's. And they wondered if they could cross the ice instead of walking on the shore, the long way round. Cross the mouth of the harbour where the ice breaks up early, chipped teeth grinning from shore to shore.

So we said to a man who was standing there, "Do you think we could cross over there now?" And he said, "Aw I think so. Take this stick and you can sort of pound on the ice as you walk and you can judge for yourself." So we did.

Her lipstick was worn off from talking and the crust of ice was as calm as the kitchen floor. Before they were married, before they moved to St. John's. Before the boys left the door banging open in the wind, racing home from Larch Place Park, before the house on Elizabeth Avenue glinted tinsel through the front room window. When her waist was still as narrow as the length of his fingers wrapped around it, when their bootprints were in step and their path was swirled by the ocean wind. When there was no way they wouldn't both see their future sons grow taller than them.

And we hit the ice like that and then we'd take a step and then we'd take another step, and no lights on, only the snow was bright.

In thirty years, he will be on his back on a bed of ice, its cold passing through his coat like a door opening beneath him. Shards in his jaw, and shards in his chest, fishing rods abandoned in the snow beside him. Above him, the clouds will bunch across the sky until he thinks he is standing on a hill, looking down at the ballycater floating across the cove. His son running through the woods from the hole in the ice to the highway for help.

And so we got over like that, and we knew it wasn't too safe and that's why we had the stick. And gosh, the next morning it was all water.

She grew up hopping on ice pans without knowing how to swim. She had her first swimming lesson at the age of sixty-six, because on her annual winter trips to Florida she would see her friends having so much fun in the pool. And then she found that she was afraid of the water, the clear warm pool, the visible white bottom.

SUNLIGHT

NANNY: My mother died when I was two.

POPPY: Yes but then you had a stepmother—

NANNY: Yes I had a stepmother—

AUNTY ALICE: —when she was eight.

NANNY: I was eight, eight years old? My father remarried when I was eight years old.

AUNTY ALICE: And in between, we had Grandmother Godley look after us, after Mother died, for I don't know how long, wasn't very long before she died. After that, Nanny Lever would come over and we had a maid, then Nanny Lever and Grandfather Lever come to live with us.

NANNY: What's her name?

AUNTY ALICE: Whose name?

NANNY: That, that maid, first maid we had? You have a better memory than I do.

ALICE: I don't know, we had so many.

ME: And what did your father do?

POPPY: Travelling salesman.

NANNY: Hardware, hardware for how many years?

ALICE: I don't remember how many years.

POPPY: Well he was at it when he was eighty years old. He was working.

ALICE: He started down to Martin Hardware.

POPPY: Fifty years travelling. At least fifty years.

NANNY: Everybody knew him! "Billy Lever, Billy Lever!"

POPPY: Oh yes.

NANNY: All across the country.

POPPY: Even today you'd go out and—

NANNY: Everybody knew him.

POPPY: —somebody would say something about Billy Lever. "Oh yes, Billy, we called him Billy."

ALICE: Very outgoing. I don't know where they got me.

NANNY: I wonder where they got you!

ALICE: I don't know, I guess Harold was that way too.

NANNY: There was no fun in ya.

ALICE: No.

NANNY: Never tell a joke…

POPPY: She crawled out from under a rock!

NANNY: There was one good thing about her, though. Often we'd all go up to LeMarchant Road, you know, boys and girls, and then you'd pair off, you know. Comin' down then, she'd always wait by the candy store on the corner, you or Harold, and then come home together so Mother never knew who I was in love with! Oh my! Fun and games.

ALICE: Lots of boyfriends.

NANNY: I was a good girl.

POPPY: Yes but nobody ever found out what you were good for!

NANNY: Well you did, you asked me to marry ya! Oh gee, I'll get you for that.

It is more than a decade since this was recorded. All three are gone now, yet their voices fill my head like my own.

Nanny always beeps when I hug her, always jumps at her own bionic sound. The whine cuts through the cloud of quiet like a needle through cloth, trailing the thread of the room.

She has found sound inside her own head, baffled by grey curls. She knows the rhythm of the spoon in the cup by heart. Her husband's mitres and jigs in the garage as he builds clocks and tea trolleys. Her children fighting in the hall. The house's winter breath, the creak of its jaw. A voice that says, wake up now, Nellie, time for school.

Every time I stay here, the first night I hear my grandfather's clock chime the hours, and the second night I don't hear it at all.

Cigar smoke warms the chilly spring air. Baymen back from the ice crowd the station, shouldering their packs and their lice. Fortune seekers bound for Cape Breton share stories of mines brimming with black cash, pulling cases packed with bravado.

Billy's case is packed with nails of different sizes. He will take them to Port Rexton, Wood Spur, Port Union Junction, Catalina. He will take them into Tilley's store, and O'Flaherty's, balancing his gab on their fine points. He will sleep in a boarding house, or with a family whose price includes breakfast and a supper called tea: beef frosted with fat, briny cabbage. Paying in cash and news from the city.

He was one of them, once, these boys heading to Boston and the General Electric plant, the high steel of New York. Sixteen and full of his brother's stories of cities with buildings tall as thirty masts, of pockets bulged with bills.

Before the war had settled on the world, turning young men's heads toward Europe. He was one of them, too—twenty-four and lured by the stories of honour and glory for King and Country. He still bears the scar along his belly from the doctor's knife, the appendicitis that saved him from the First Five Hundred of the Newfoundland Regiment, which fell almost to a man at Beaumont Hamel. Saved from that ridge in France, he had found himself in Alexandria, and Suvla Bay, and then buried alive in the trench mud where his friends had fought and died three years before. He carries these things, too: heads pounded down into the trenches, bodies rusted with blood. Memories threaded to deepen into flesh.

All aboard that's goin aboard, and the cigar stub drops into his breast pocket, cushioned in ash.

Would like to know about the family of Kizziah Harmon, wife of William Lever. Their son John Wade Belton Lever is buried at ... I'm looking for Charles Hopper who worked for Lever Brother Soaps in the 1930s on the West Coast. Any connections...

My Uncle Les has spent years on the family tree, plotting it out like a map as if you could follow it to the past: Billy Lever, to William Senior, to James, to Richard, b. 1780. Stops where you can rest a while, take off your boots, along the road to Port Sunlight on the shore of the Mersey.

Somehow we are related to that other William Lever, Lord Leverhulme of England, founder of Lever Brothers, of Sunlight and Vim, who named the company town after his soap. Born the same year as my great-great-grandfather, also William, also son of James, like the Levers of a parallel universe. Probably never called Billy in his life.

My Great Aunt Alice tells quiet tales of a letter from England, how her grandfather saw Port Sunlight on the return address and threw the letter in the fire, unopened. If they wanted to contact us, he said, they should have done it years ago. Whispers become lore, of a will, an unclaimed inheritance.

Uncle Les follows the Williams, the Jameses, along the fine threads of the web, through dusty books, across oceans. He walks through the Lady Lever Art Gallery, looking for a different kind of fortune: that intake of breath that comes when you see yourself in the distant past.

Like holding a map whose rivers trace the shape of a face.

I am searching for a Yhost Lever (b:1800) who came from Germany thru Pennsylvania to Indiana and then Michigan ... Searching for my paternal grandfather, Henry Lever Ferguson, who is believed to have died in Canada about 1939...

Billy rides the train to its farthest reaches, through the Topsail mountains—even mountains speak of ships—up tidal grades, through squalls of snow, across the plateau at Gaff Topsails, the section that has stranded trains for weeks in snow drifts two stories high, derailing even rescuers.

It is raining in St. John's. He can hear it in the knock of the car along the track, in the sound of a child crying in a distant berth. His children are tucked in at home by Jenny's grieving mother and a maid he hired in an afternoon.

When he returns, he'll tell them tales of the giant red plow on the engine that shovels through the snow, the whole train reversing and then ramming at the mound, pitching the passengers back and forth, piling the banks up higher and higher on either side till the train is tunnelling through a planet of snow.

Days of nothing but dark through the windows. Like riding off the edge of the earth.

My mother was named for two grandmothers, not maternal and paternal, but living and ghost, mother and dream. A genealogy told when I was a child: Elizabeth for her mother's stepmother, Jenny for Jenny Godley, the mother who had died when my grandmother was small enough to wait for her by the door, and small enough finally to forget.

Jenny Godley is a whisper, the fascination and the horror of first learning that your mother can die. Never just Jenny, never Jenny Lever, always Jenny Godley, her maiden name in one breath.

A name for an angel smiling sadly on a Christmas card. Restored to maidenhood, princess on a bier, mermaid turned to foam.

Where's the baby?
What baby?
Your baby.
I don't have a baby, Nanny. You must be thinking of Colleen.

Ah, yes.

Wasn't too bad, I s'pose. A lot luckier than a lot of people who lost their parents. But Dad saw that we were well looked after, when he was gone always. But Grandfather died, so my grandmother came over. So we had a housemaid and then the servant girl, see, doing work. They let the housemaid go, and Nanny used to make sure that she was there overseeing everything, you know, she had to 'cause my grandfather died, so we had her come over that winter to stay.

I can't follow the chronology. A collection of caregivers and deaths—not a line of train cars, following one after the other; but the snow beyond the window, white upon white upon white. She was too small to remember, and now she is old enough to forget. Her mother, and Grandmother Godley. Whispers of other losses—Uncle Jim and his wife who had died somewhere in Massachusetts. Jim's orphaned children who had been sent back to live with their grandparents in Newfoundland, until the girl died of pneumonia, until the boy fell off the fishing stage.

This is what she remembers: Nanny Lever's cane always set to crack against their legs if they passed too near. That kind maid who kicked the rug wet with pee beneath the bed so that her grandmother wouldn't see. Who let them watch the cat play with a mouse in its paws.

During the summers, their friends went to visit cousins down around the bay, to fish and pick berries, while she and her siblings stayed in St. John's, no cousins to visit. And when Grandfather Lever passed away, the other kids in the neighbourhood refused to enter the haunted house on Bannerman Street.

Elizabeth Churchill is the Matron. Married now to the new hospital and its heavy browed dormers, married to care and cleanliness, to her nurses' good comportment. Her old house was sold to the hospital after her husband died, and dragged across the Tickle ice to be the doctor's residence. Now she sees it from the nurses' cottage, watches Dr. Parsons pull out walls and build a sun porch cased in sparkling glass.

The patients come in skiffs from across Notre Dame Bay, from Herring Neck, Musgrave Harbour, La Scie. They come with their hooked fingers white with infection, their broken bones, the lungers with their blood-soaked handkerchiefs. Those with no money bring vegetables, and berries picked on the hills, to be preserved and spooned into the patients' chapped mouths come winter.

She watches over the nurses as they sharpen needles on an oil stone, boil instruments and the TB patients' dishes. She wipes the pink spittle from her patients' chins as she had done for her husband, when the nearest hospital was in St. Anthony. His cough, then, like the coughs of these strangers, foreign and wild, running like a frightened horse. She will soothe them as she did him, and bathe their naked bodies, all limp, all thin.

Billy comes from Lewisporte on the *Clyde*, like a letter someone mailed her, tucked between the supplies from St. John's. New wounds for her healing hands, new souls to salve. She will be his matron, now. She will follow him back to the city, on the steamer and the rail lines, like a new hammer in his case ready to smooth old nail heads.

This man will give her the children that God never did, already grown near as tall as her, but growing still in other ways. She will rely on duty until she loves them. They will care for the porch steps, and make their beds; she will train them. Faces starched and fingernails cut clean. No one questions if the children will call her Mother.

When Aunty Alice comes down the hall, Nanny says, *Uh oh, here comes the teacher.* And it could be a joke, a jab at her prim older sister, at this childhood that has come back to her like fog rolling in over the Narrows. No one asks.

My mother makes an album for her of all her grandchildren, and points at the pictures like a text book, our nine faces flashing like multiplication tables, like French nouns. From birth through awkward grades, pictures of apple cheeks, *la pomme.*

I don't want to know these stories. I want to know the first childhood, I want nickel street car rides and faking sick to watch a matinee at the Capitol Theatre, Water Street ladies in hats with blue ribbon, stray goats in the streets. Fog like putting on a hat.

Elizabeth dreams of fire, waking soaked in water from the fire engines—her own sweat. In the attic are three children who would have two wooden staircases to descend, as flames spread along the row-houses like a ball rolling down a hill. As they did in '92 when a match in a hay loft flattened two-thirds of the city, burning through the homes of thousands, through the shops on Water Street and the wharves, stopped only by the water of the harbour. The flames would have no more respect for the thin walls between the row-houses of Bannerman Street than the maid, who stands in the kitchen with her ear to the wall, cheeks burning at the sound of the Mick neighbours saying their rosary. It is too close, this city, too thick with smoke and prejudice carried in coats from Ireland. She can smell the neighbour's bathwater, taste their fish through her bedroom window. Feel the heat of their bodies and their flames.

Snowed in
my mother brings her paper,
writes down the words Nanny cannot hear.

You look nice in purple.

It's windy.

This is a meeting of the Ladies Auxiliary
homemade squares and strong tea,
Thank you all for coming this afternoon.

My mother digs, the pen
a poor tool for wet snow.
What is my name?
Elizabeth Noseworthy.
What is my married name?

Outside, the lilacs are blooming, so it must be summer.
In her hand is a flower stem, small lettered petals.
This coat is too big, it must be Fraser's.

What kind of flower?
Petunia?
Nanny not sure.

She nods to her guests, there is work to be done.
It is cold and soon it will be Christmas.

Where is Jean?

Where is home?

Alberta.

The minutes will be passed.
She can nod and pretend she has heard every word.
Thank you daughters for the visit and the cooking.

NANNY: He'd be gone all week but he always made sure he got home on the weekends. He'd take us to church in the morning, and then we had to go to Sunday school in the afternoon, and when we come home from Sunday school you had to have your little nap then. He'd be ready for us, and he'd all take us by the hand, Al and I and Harold, the three of us, and go down to the cemetery. Ugh! But we went anyway because Dad was such a good sport, he liked to talk and tell you things. I miss that too. Oh my, and when I think about it—I often think about the times we used to have. And the children, they're never satisfied, they got everything now and they're still not satisfied, well, we were satisfied with things.

POPPY: C'mon honey, your milk is ready.

NANNY: Wha?

POPPY: Your milk is ready.

NANNY: You milked a cow, did ya?

POPPY: Yes, I did.

I find her on this tape when silence has become a place.

Where it is Saturday night, and her new mother joins the others along Bannerman Street calling their children in for their baths. Fake lemon and steam. Parade of skin pinked from hot water and scrubbing.

Where her grandmother sits up in bed as she brings her hot water, her concentration rippling the surface of the bowl. Where she does sums at the table. Where cigar smoke sweetens the walls.

Her head sinks into memory, a child in the bath finding giant squid and sunken ships. My voice inaudible, my face blurred in pale blue light.

And each house along the empty street is filled with the smell of Sunlight soap — the laundry and the floor, the porch steps and the children all scrubbed shiny and raw from that blue and yellow box.

SENSE

ME: How did you meet?

POPPY: Oh, out to church. We went to the same church, see.

NANNY: Young people's school, you know.

POPPY: You had the Young People's Association, and you'd meet every Tuesday night—

NANNY: We went to Sunday school, and then we'd talk, at Sunday school,

POPPY: —and we'd play games, and that kind of stuff, and you'd go to Sunday school,

NANNY: Went to Sunday school, and I taught the—

POPPY: Of course you had to go to church.

NANNY: ... And after that I went into the choir. And after that, I married that old fella. Some old now, I tell ya!

He called her honey like he meant just that—a slow familiar sweetness. She couldn't hear it but could see it, golden in his mouth, in his eye.

And sometimes, sure, he would shout, a different shout from the one for her hearing aid—*Who are all the eggs for sure it's just the two of us You can't put on your fur coat it's the middle of the goddamn summer and where are you going?*

The nurses and the children came, but he put in her hearing aid, the only one who knew how to change the batteries, how to fit it right. The tender ritual: lifting back her brumey curls to set the case, gentle turn of mould into her ear, fingers on her cheek, breath in her hair.

When the hand soap had to be hidden so she couldn't put it in the dishwasher, he cleaned the house, learned to cook and managed to put the sewing machine needle through his thumb. She still wagged her finger when he told a dirty joke, sensing the punchline. If she could hear it she'd have topped it. And for a while they still sat at the table, breathing bergamot and the peace of a marriage six decades long.

They got her a room in the Agnes Pratt, a double, so if that other lady dies—But once he'd tucked her in the quilt from home, he started letting go of the things that he had made last, patched and darned: his kidneys, his heart.

And no one knew if she understood the news shouted in her ear. They found food in her mouth hours after lunch, rolling on her tongue like she was trying to match a taste to a memory.

After he died, her doctor said that he had told him years ago—she had no hearing left at all. No point in keeping the hearing aid in.

THE STEPPING-OFF PLACE

On my grandfather's wall
the framed baptismal certificate
of an older brother, outlived
by eighty years.

Only six months old
when his small breath caught

          like a sleeve on a nail.
Red eyes, spots inside his tiny mouth
a spreading stain across his skin.

In this family tree
my great-grandmother's limb
bears more fragile things:
                                        a leaf,
                                                an egg.

Or her body is scrub
low to the ground,
    braced against wind
      with tender tubers reaching
                  into earth.

On my grandfather's wall
a photo of his brother Leslie
in his British Royal Navy uniform,
the words
      For King and Country
      Killed in Action.

Only twenty-four years old
when his young breath caught

   in his throat,
watching the swarm of Luftwaffe
a spreading stain across the sky.

My grandfather keeps these papers
reminding him that he too
is a sprout,
    an eye,
       a small thing cut from flesh.

Leaves that make him stop,
listen to his own breath.

Have mercy on us down in Newfoundland, we are but a fog-shrouded rock in the North Atlantic.
—Joey Smallwood, 1947

The tide goes out, and the land swells like a lung.
Erratics sit on the roadside, as if waiting for the glaciers that left them to return.

Some call it The Rock.

My grandfather tells of the boyhood friend who jumped over the gap in the cliff path, how rock and body gave way, gushed into the deep water below as my grandfather watched, his own body already leaning forward to follow. Even stone is fluid.

My grandfather tells of the farm beneath the gas station, the pond filled in by the road. Of the rock that held potatoes and cabbages, the tendrils of carrot tops teasing the shy orange skin below ground.

In an Alberta restaurant, eating mussels in white wine I get sand between my teeth, rock worn by water. Rock so fine that in the context of sun, it could be called soft under your toes.

The pond used to freeze over—course we'd make a skating rink. Shovel the snow off and we'd go down there skating, and used to be crowds of people come in from town, they'd come in for skating on the pond, on the ice... A hundred feet from the house.

Leslie was six years older than Fraser, an adult, when adulthood was a distant green country. They milked with numb fingers in the fog of their breath, and in summer worked side by side in the fields, pulling weeds or making hay, and swam in the pond in the heat of the afternoon, perhaps trying to dunk each other, and maybe smoking a cigarette, and talking about girls. Leslie probably giving advice, teaching how to throw a punch, and take one, racing across the pond—of course letting his kid brother win. Just a kid too, really. Fraser does not speak of this.

What he remembers now, to his granddaughter listening, is the water, the way the clean cool met his hot dusty face, the way the surface held the ripple, when a diver dropped to the bottom.

We'd go down there fishing—it had all sorts of trout into it, and a river running in and a river running out. Our swimming hole was right in the mouth of the river running in. And all the summer we'd be down there.

And in the nighttime, we'd be out sitting on the veranda, and you'd see the moon shining on the water, you know? It was beautiful. That pond was the life of the place.

The Newfoundland Butter Company bore the first neon sign in Newfoundland, a giant cow that glowed above the entrance as the workers filed in on dark winter mornings. The Newfoundland Butter Company didn't even make butter.

Thomas Noseworthy was a farmer who made oleomargarine, "Good Luck" and "Eversweet." He left his sons to milk the cows and drove to town, entered beneath the neon bovine to a steady wage and the promise of a pension, the first in Newfoundland.

In distant Canada, the dairy farmers kept the cheap fat from kitchen tables by law, enshrined in the British North America Act. But Newfoundland's few cows made butter a golden spread, a fancy import from far away places, and margarine meant jobs. Bootleg margarine was smuggled into Canada, dyed yellow. It would sit between Newfoundland and Canada on the negotiating table after the war: Newfoundland would join Canada if they could keep making margarine; Canada would welcome them if they did not sell it off the island.

The men at the Butter Company made the margarine with a little milk mixed with seal oil, heated in giant vats, emulsified, then cooled and congealed, the fishy odour of hot churning seal oil haunting their bread. There is no irony, then, in my great-grandfather's career. In this country without enough butter, he collected his pay and went home to sweet fresh cream churned with an egg beater at the table.

He pits the fish offal, the sour manure and turf warming the fall chill, ploughing it all into the bog for the winter to spread on the fields in the spring.

(He once told me, city girl, girl of a new century, of thinning vegetables, the picking, the picking rocks. I saw an old man bending in the furrows).

He heaves up the shovel thinking of *Richard III*. He can see Richard's winter in his breath, and thinks of corrupt kings and rumours of war.

(I have the small brown copies of his English schoolbooks with their softened cloth corners and his precise teenage handwriting: *Fraser Noseworthy, September 13th, 1938*).

By spring, the pit will be ripe to fertilize the vegetables and hay, by spring, the Germans will have invaded Czechoslovakia and signed a pact with fascist Italy. By July, he will be seventeen and finished high school. He'll put away his math book, his *Richard III* and *English, Spoken and Written,* he'll help his brother to spread the bog that steeped all winter across the fields, and wait.

At dusk, three schooners grappled the chain with their anchors, and the capstan heaved it from the bottom of the Harbour. Fort Waldegrave and Fort Amherst, Chain Rock and Pancake Rock, linked by iron that, from ships, looked like thread across the Narrows. It was 1770, and the chain would hold back the French, along with the shot furnaces that burned to load the cannons with fire.

The chain became a net, the schooners minesweepers, the warships submarines. The eighteenth century became the twentieth, and the French became the Germans. Corvettes and destroyers in the Newfoundland Escort Force huddled before the convoy across the North Atlantic. The Constabulary confiscated rolls of film with children posed in front of the Narrows. The Canadian War Cabinet's plan for German invasion was to sink the ships to block the port, fill the harbour with ten thousand tonnes of fuel drained from the tanks on the Southside Hills, and light the city on fire.

Not the hinterland, not a half hour into the sea, but the very front of North America. The gateway to a continent, the stepping-off place.

It burns every hour of the day, the stove in the hall. The one in the kitchen from dawn until bedtime. They burn and his shoulders burn, and he dreams of chopping wood, chopping from dawn until bedtime, chopping every hour of the day. In the fall, he and Leslie and his father had hauled the trees from the woods behind the house to prepare for this, the winter and the insatiable stoves. And on Saturdays they prepare for Sundays, chopping double to last the day of rest.

In the morning, before the dark has lifted off the fields, he will milk the cows in the white fog of his own breath. And it will be worth it, then, the smell of smoke after the barn, the promise of numb fingers warming over the dry cast-iron heat, of tea strong as ink swirled with his own fresh cream. And in the hot kitchen his brother will tease him, punching his arms thickening with new muscle, the arms now of a man, his cheeks proud and burning like a boy's.

During the war, everything was blacked out.

No lights, never saw a light anywhere. You couldn't walk along the street and light a cigarette. And the cars, the cars had a hood over the headlights. And we had shutters on the windows, so you couldn't see any light outside at all. See, it was the stepping-off place to North America, as you can well imagine.

A German submarine sailed up Conception Bay. And the big high cliffs on Bell Island, they had guns up there. And I understand they tried to fire at this submarine, but they couldn't deflect the guns low enough, so the crew came right in under the cliffs. And there were two boats tied up there waiting to take iron ore, and they were torpedoed, sunk right there. And that's right in the bay, you know?

All around the coast, they were swarming with German submarines.

Leslie enlisted with the British Royal Navy, was stationed on the minesweeper *Abronia*. An Ordinary Seaman. She was an old fishing trawler from Grimsby. But he was a Newfoundlander from a farm, and she was no longer after fish. Her lines were set with paravenes that stretched out wide at port and stern to slice the mines from their moorings. When a horned head bobbed to the surface, he handed shells to the sharpshooters trying to pierce its skull and gently sink it to the ocean floor. If they hit the trigger the mine, he knew, would explode in a maw of shrapnel and water. All hands put on their lifebelts as the trawler entered the grid.

He knew that other things lurked too, silently beneath them: U-boats that could dive in thirty seconds, slipping under the escorts; magnetic mines that had no cables but sent shock waves from the bottom; acoustic mines that waited for the trembling of a hull.

After all this, it was the dock that was deadly, and the sky and not the sea that swallowed the trawler at port, sitting still in east London. What did the young Newfoundlander on patrol think when he looked up and saw the 300 Luftwaffe bombers rolling in, a black fog of planes with their 300 tonnes of bombs for London? More planes than anyone had ever seen, descending on a city that lay anchored to the earth, pointing anti-aircraft fire at a storm. Twenty-four years old, he would not see as night fell blacked-out London alight with fire, misnamed Black Saturday. The first night of the Blitz. It was four months after he left home.

His father was paid $8.17 for the "residue" of his wages, the residue of his body pulled from the water and buried in Communal Grave No. 1 in East London Cemetery, with the four other ratings who died on the ship, and the dead from the burned-out convent, the school-turned-shelter. The *Abronia* would be raised from the Thames a year later, while the bombs cremated their bodies in the ground.

Residue of Naval Assets.

In the case of Derrick Leslie Nosworthy deceased.

In reply quote—

No. D.N.A. (Wills) 6348/1940

Admiralty, D.N.A. (Wills),
Bath, Somerset.

and address letter to—
The Inspector of Seamen's Wills,
Admiralty, D.N.A. (Wills),
Bath,
Somerset.

10 April, 1941

Sir,

I have to inform you that your claim as Father of the above-named deceased has been admitted, and that payment will be made to you in due course.

I have to add that you are bound to administer this estate according to law, and that a Certificate, authorizing you to do so, will be forwarded with the order for payment. The directions on the other side of this form (~~No.~~) should be carefully noted.

The deceased's Service Certificate is enclosed herewith. ~~forwarded in support of your claim~~ ~~returned herewith.~~

1.

I am, Sir,
Your obedient Servant,
T. J. WINNALL
~~H. EBORALL,~~
Inspector of Seamen's Wills.

Mr H. J. Nosworthy.

I.S.W. Form No. 12 727 Wt 27058/3360 2000 10/40 F.A. Gp. 698

The American and Canadian soldiers wanted Newfoundland's milk and fresh meat and vegetables. And they wanted Newfoundland's farms for forts and barracks and runways. And they wanted Newfoundland's men to build them, and they would pay a quarter of what they paid their own, and it would still be more money than the Newfoundlanders had ever seen. The forts and bases wanted Newfoundland's men, and the war wanted Newfoundland's men. And the farmer's sons went to Europe to fight, and many would not come home. And all the tractors and milking machines that the Canadians' money could buy would not bring them home, to help with the harvest in the fall, to stand beside their fathers and brothers pitching hay into the loft. To wash the sweat off their backs in the swimming hole at the mouth of the river.

Fraser and Millie were always too much alike to like each other, siblings in their eighties bickering like kids over whether their bread was called "buns" or "rolls." *They're not buns, you sit on your buns!* Millie just as stubborn, *Dad in a skirt*, her nieces said.

He hadn't forgotten the time she returned home from Calgary with her new husband—the Canuck in his Cadillac with the antler hood ornament, showing off. Those Calgarians with their ten-gallon hats and their pint-size brains.

He hadn't forgotten how the Canadians had built the air base on farms in Torbay, how the Canadian troops stationed here were classed as serving "overseas," while the Newfoundlanders, still bleeding from Beaumont Hamel, signed up to fight for Mother England and were shipped off to North Africa.

He hadn't forgotten his city a few years later, draped in black in mourning for the country, stolen, he said, in backroom dealings between imperialists with different accents.

Millie squints in her bright Calgary sun, says, *There were never any antlers on that car!*

The U-boats had sunk the *Caribou*—a ferry of civilians sailing to Sydney. Families thrown from their bunks by the torpedo blast, then throwing themselves into the icy sea. A vessel of the same class as the one he takes to his post in Labrador. There is a woman on board who sees a periscope, a finger crooked toward her across the water. The captain tells her she is wrong, it couldn't be, even as he pulls the ship in to a sheltered bay for the night.

One in the family is enough, they had told him when he tried to join the Air Force. Though he knew families with more enlisted, with more lost. Though he knew that one was, in fact, too many. He took night classes in wireless telegraphy, traded the cows for weather stations in Labrador. They call it Battle Harbour, the place where he is stationed, though it is miles from the battles of Europe and his brother's battered body. Named for a forgotten war between the Montagnais and the Inuit.

He awakes in the middle of the night to a bright light sweeping across the ship like a slow, hot hand. He waits, barely breathing, as if they will hear him through the steel hulls. He waits for the torpedo that does not come, that they do not waste on this boat. The next morning, a convoy of Allied ships nearby is sunk by submarines. 137 dead on the *Caribou*, who knows how many more on this morning's convoy. And he is alive. And he is not on the escort ships, not speeding through the section of Atlantic called "the Pit," two miles above a graveyard of Allied ships. Not watching the glow of London burning.

Battle of the Atlantic. Battle Harbour.

Who, now, will shovel the bog and seal blubber onto the land. Who will seed the potatoes with a knife, who will milk the cows when the morning tastes of fog and the barn is warmed by manure and breath. Who will haul the hay, pulling the chaff from shirt cuffs. Who will pluck carrots the width of veins from their rows, while the Canadians rumble over the road. Who will chop the wood. And who will chop it tomorrow.

Who will swim in the pond, when the evening light silvers the surface, so that you worry a moment that your dive into glass will cut you on the way down.

Mother would be out to church, just about every night, Women's Association meetings, all that kind of thing. And he'd be home sitting in the little living room all night long by himself. After leaving the farm which was his pride and joy. And I didn't realize, you know, what that would do to him. I didn't realize what that was doing to him. Because he just sat there in this room, and he used to love to go out and walk around the fields, you know, and look at the crops when he'd come home from work in the night.

The new house on Cavell Avenue has running water and central heating, and a wall that it shares with the neighbours, and a squat yard that overlooks the pool of rain in the street. Here he will wait out the war.

She sees their son's ghost, but he does not. He listens to the lowing of neighbours. He listens to the bleat of the traffic. And after the war, when the Canadians and Americans head home with their Newfie wives, he keeps marching to work, though production has been cut in half, though the neon cow was taken down during the blackouts.

In his belly is a sickness that the company doctor calls a persistent flu. From his bed he can hear the neighbours fighting, making love, while sacs on his bowel grow with poison, like cow vetch in the furrows, like ringworm on cattle's flanks. Just a flu, until she finds him on the bathroom floor.

Peritonitis, someone says. But they will not operate because of his angina. His wife and two of his children are at his side.

He'd come home from one job and he'd get something to eat and he'd go out on the grounds and he was working then till dark. And on Sundays then he'd go walking around, and 'twas his life. He was looking forward to retiring on this, and he sold it, got rid of it. And I didn't know the difference. You know, didn't realize the difference, what it was doing to him.

Finally someone finds a surgeon who is willing to operate, since it is his only chance. The surgery is scheduled for the following morning at eight o'clock. He dies at three.

There was a man moved in, he bought the property next to us, and most of that pond was on his land. Now, we weren't there anymore, we were living out in town then, but he got bulldozers in and he dozed out the river. And drained the pond. And it was a shame because it was the life living in there you know, without that, without that pond there…

I think if we were living there we would have protested that, but Dad sold the farm and sold the house, and the people that bought it never moved in, he rented it. So 'twas nobody to protest.

And they tell me when he let it drain, and all the water was gone, they tell me the fish were flapping on the bottom.

THE NEW ROAD

A*ND THEN WE'D COD JIG, in the summertime. And Pop knew all the places to go. He knew where every shoal was, every rock was, up and down that arm.*

Whenever you talked about *Little Heart's Ease,* I thought you were saying Little Heart Seas. I could see the outport facing the sea, clasping the fingertips of the Southwest Arm. The sea defined that place for a girl who had only been there once, who had always lived 1000 kilometres inland. Who could not find the ocean in waves of wheat.

You showed me your grandparents' house, the beach, with your wineglass, your fork and knife. Napkin for the bay, pepper for Caplin Cove, hand spread for the line of the harbour. *Heart's Ease was here*, at the tender crook of your thumb. Sunday plates cleared from the table and it is summer down around the bay, your eyes bright in the sun with Pop showing you, *drop the line to the bottom, two arm lengths up, and away you go*, jigging your memories to hook me with flashes of light. Arms reaching above your head—*you had to hold it up like this… cause if you did it like this, you'd get a face full of water.*

The wharves, the stage, the boat, speech and memories rolling faster now, calling it by *Heartsease*, run together in a single word with stress on the first syllable, and easy as the shaker of salt, you pass me your nostalgia.

It was a five-hour trip from your home in St. John's to your grandparents' house. Before the TransCanada the narrow dirt road to Heart's Ease followed the coastline, and if it rained, your dad's baby blue Meteor sank in mud up to the axles. When the rain froze, the car fishtailed up the slope. *And I remember that Chapel Arm and Norman's Cove was like a welcome relief. Two small communities and they weren't quite half way. But okay, you're getting there.* Your father approached the blind corners blowing the horn, the road wrapping the cliffs like a window ledge. The Meteor inching along it, as if deciding whether to jump. Your father making everyone get out of the car before he tried to climb the frozen slope, then waiting for you to walk up the hill when he got to the top.

And Chapel Arm, Norman's Cove, you don't even drive through them now because they're on the coast. Goobies with its chip stand in the summer, huddling beneath the awning out of the rain. Queen's Cove. Long Beach. Island Cove, below the road, slope of saltbox roofs and gardens grown over with thistle. *And you could look down and you'd see the houses—nobody living there, but you could see the houses.* Every time you watched for it, the ghost town, the place so like Heart's Ease, slipping past the backseat window.

This was the entrance to the arm, and here was a little outport called House Cove.

In 1949, Joey Smallwood had become the first premier of Newfoundland. He said he would "drag Newfoundlanders kicking and screaming into the twentieth century," he said, "Burn your boats." He dreamed of glove factories and cement plants, of towns with the sweet smell of chocolate masking the sea. He said, "Develop or perish." He gave families a few hundred dollars to move to his growth centres, where they fought for the fishing grounds. In two decades, 300 outports were gone.

The big excitement was when the L___s, were going to be getting this house from House Cove. House Cove must have been abandoned about ten years before this. So the house was still in reasonably good shape—may have needed a coat of paint, but you know these people didn't have any other income. And so the trick was to get it out.

They put logs beneath the foundation, and chopped the house from its pilings. Horses and men pulled the house toward the water, and more men slowed it with ropes from behind. The logs left behind were dragged around front to meet the threshold. It took a full day to get the house to the beach. Then they hitched it to the boats waiting off shore, like putting a leash on an old dog.

When the house went in the water, it sank, it must have been about three feet. I remember—aw geez I remember it to this day because the water was about maybe halfway up the door. And I'll never forget, I said, is she gonna sink? Is she gonna sink? And my grandfather—no no, she'll just drop down about three feet, b'y, and she'll level off.

House Cove, like a strange discount store, a used house lot. If you lived here you'd already be home.

You tell me of going out across the arm in Pop's sixteen-foot open boat, looking, even then, for signs of bad weather. How when whitecaps crested the horizon you would get up in the fore-cuddy, where the bow was planked across the gunnels, where there was just enough room for a small boy to hide amongst the jiggers from the waves. Even in the foulest weather, Pop would be smiling and whistling, while you did the worrying for you both. *If Pop pulled up the oilskin, I knew we were in for it.*

Stories of stories, heard jigging in an open boat. The fishing trip when Pop jumped into the Atlantic to save his buddy from drowning, then headed for the nearest bit of beach, lit a fire with gasoline, and sat shivering naked in the snow, bright white bodies aglow while they roasted their oilskins like marshmallows. Sailing his schooner through the St. John's Narrows in the middle of a storm, how as the wind caught the sails, the boom came around and broke his leg. How Nan ran the wireless station in Heart's Ease, and got the message in a slow trail of dashes and dots. *Pop would go out in a hurricane.* Stories of a WWI commando, of putting ashore in a rubber boat with a 303 Enfield, of a soldier in Halifax on December 6th, 1917, when the harbour exploded. Fragments of running towards the city, of people without limbs, of rubble and smoke.

And the old salts chuckling on the beach, saying, *You aren't going out in this now, are ya Skipper?*

Pop wrote poems that he did not keep.
His poems were paper planes
made of rhyme and the adventures of an afternoon
        landing at your feet with a laugh—
        that it flew so fast, that the nose brushed Dad's hair.

Each spring he scraped the old paint off the skiff:
See the gaps here between the planks
poke in the oakum with the chisel
then we'll seal her up tight with pitch and paint.
He taught you the rhythm
of pitch and oakum,
the value of the line of rough hemp.
Make sure you do it right
you don't want to be out in the bay
when the oakum comes out.

There are no poems left now
from this man who died before I was born.
I'll never hear the timbre of his voice—
only yours, reciting the smell of pitch,
        the hewn of the hull,
        the pleasure of hearing your own name
        rhymed with the afternoon's lunch
        before he puts the poem in the fire.

St. Jones Without was abandoned around the time that you were born. It sits outside Random Sound, while its favoured sister, St. Jones Within, keeps its residents tucked in the northern sleeve of the Arm.

Without the Sound, without sound, save the flap of clapboard and gulls whose only garbage comes from the sea. Without the smell of seal flipper pie, without shirts on the line. Without skiffs but one docked by pillaging pirates, Viking explorers.

At first, you are hushed too, like entering a church. Then you loosen again into your pirate stances, breaking windows because you can, fighting for roles of sheriff and outlaw, standoffs with driftwood guns. Scaring yourselves with ghost stories and the flutter of birds in the attic beams. Till the shadows stretch and your bellies growl, and everyone has been killed in the shootout. And the houses seem like bones scraped of meat, the hollowed rooms like playing inside a skull. And you long for your mothers and the fishiness of seal sealed in gravy and pie crust. To fold yourself within Pop's voice and Nan's arms, and pretend you are too old for kisses from your grandmother.

Racing for the boat, yanking on the fly-wheel, your arms still as skinny as the cord.

Pop knew where there was a stand of trees tall enough to build a new wharf, pilings long enough to drive them deep into the ocean floor to bear the sea ice. Near Island Cove, where there was a creek bed to float the timbers down to the water, where they could be leashed to the skiff and pulled down the arm to Heart's Ease. Where no one lived anymore to claim them.

The TransCanada had been finished in 1965, and there wasn't much reason to drive by Island Cove anymore. The new road channelled through woods, away from the water, and the trip was easy now, when you had time to make it. Had you met my mother yet, that summer you built the new wharf? Were you already dreaming of med school? Of me?

You and Pop and your dad and brothers spent the day felling trees for the new wharf. But when you set out for home the raft, dragging behind the skiff like a stubborn dog, strained the motor and you ran out of gas. And your mother, waiting at home, saw everyone she loved drowning in the arm, even as you slowly rowed in to shore, the raft set free to drift to a nearby island. Phoning everyone she knew in places up the arm, until a man in Hodge's Cove spotted you rowing on the water. He met you on the beach, saying, *Frances phoned, she's kind of upset.*

The wharf that was built with the logs retrieved the next day is gone now. And the old house, and Nan and Pop, and the cod. But unlike House Cove and Island Cove, in Heart's Ease there is smoke from the chimneys of houses once moved across the arm. There are old folks here, and in winter, a few seals on the ice. One summer, twenty-six tonnes of hash seized from a boat by the RCMP, and in your living room in Alberta you see your grandfather's tiny outport on *The National.*

Pepper and salt are returned to the cupboard, the placemats are wiped with a too-wet cloth, leaving a trail of water beading across the plastic. *There were several communities up and down the arm—Loreburn was one, St. Jones Without was another, and House Cove, and Island Cove was another, that people were moved out.*

The turnoff to Island Cove was bulldozed after the residents left. And the path was barred, so you could never go back.

THE BOSUN CHAIR

AT NINE, SHE LEAVES HOME to become a servant in St. John's. At nine years old she leaves school, leaves her mother and father and brothers and sisters, leaves her rag-doll and other childish things. Leaves the little outport of Brooklyn in the skirts of Bonavista Bay, for the city. There is one year left in the century.

The mouth of the harbour is flanked by cliffs high as storm clouds. Sealing ships dock just inside the harbour, near the seal oil refineries. Schooners cluster in further, foresting the harbour with their masts. The waterfront is lined with wharves spread with fish, waiting for inspection, and scaffolds for drying cod arch across the streets. Around the north side of the harbour, the old city tumbles up the hills, a huddle of narrow dirt streets, wooden tenements and gothic churches. The air is thick with smoke and the dank smell of animals and humans and water.

She will become Mrs. Noseworthy to acquaintances, Mom to three, Nanny to my mother and her other grandchildren. But as she steps into this strange city she is only nine, and her name is Jean Chaulk.

It may be one of the colonial mansions on Rennie's Mill Road—crisp white porch pillars masting the doorways, twelve-foot walls jungled with wallpaper—where Jean is first sent to work for the old judge. Later there will be hints of abuse, that these days in this house are the seeds of what will become a life-long bitterness. It might be one of the mansions on Waterford Bridge Road on the west end, backing on to the Waterford River—grand staircases with mahogany newel posts reflecting the crystal chandelier light. She could not imagine that one day her grandson will live in one of these houses, restoring it to its Victorian glory.

She works sixteen-hour days for room and board and a few dollars to send back home. Jean is days away from home, and lucky for it. Lucky to be in St. John's and not working in the Boston States like so many other outport girls, closer to Brooklyn, New York, than Brooklyn, Newfoundland.

Monday: Washing. She begins the day boiling the whites with lye. She scrubs stains on a washboard, cranks the clothes through a wringer, and hangs them to dry until Tuesday.

Tuesday: Ironing. She heats the heavy sad irons on the stove, cycling through them as they cool, with breaks to stoke the fire. Sweat trickles down her back, and the heat chokes her with her own yellowed collar.

Wednesday: Baking, years of bread, cakes and scones (a secret taste of batter when her thumb pokes down into the bowl).

Thursday: Cleaning upstairs, where the summer sun spotlights the dust.

Friday: Cleaning downstairs, where the winter snow puddles on the floor.

Saturday: More baking, between the dishwashing and cooking, scrubbing the tea-stained cups with baking soda. She retreats at midnight to a draughty attic bunk, a hook for her apron behind the door. Where she will start to bleed, far away from her mother.

Sunday: A half-day rest—a book in the kitchen with her feet under the stove. Rereading a love letter before returning it to its hiding place in the hollow iron bedpost, under the loose brass knob.

Monday: Washing. She begins the day.

On the 16th of September, 1907, Jean Chaulk boarded The *Duchess of Fife*, a cargo schooner loaded with goods for a merchant in Bonavista. She was sixteen years old. Outport girls often worked in the city through the winter and came home for the summer season to help make the fish. But no one knows why Jean was returning home at this time of year. She was not returning home for good.

While Carbonear we reached that night,
And early left next morn,
To run for Catalina,
As our captain feared the storm.

The storm the captain feared was faster than the schooner, though they travelled on the same wind. Thirty miles off Catalina. The gale grew. Twenty miles, and the day was so black they might have looked for stars. Ten miles off, the *Duchess* lost her main boom, leaving her adrift on the waves.

She drifted to the Funks, the island named for the foul odour of guano left by the millions of terns and gannets that nest there. Off its southwest shore, hidden sunkers skulk beneath the water in wait for the flesh of ships' hulls. In this place, the *Duchess* began to leak with the strain of the wind and swarming waves.

Tom Noseworthy is a mason, stacking stones until whole buildings take shape beneath his hands. Maybe she falls in love with him for this; while she spends the hours scrubbing collars that will be re-soiled with sweat and baking bread that will be gobbled with one cup of tea, what he makes can withstand the worst of the Atlantic's gales. Perhaps they are to her like private monuments around the city, like secret, intimate messages that everyone can see, but of which only she knows the meaning. Perhaps she simply sees in him a way to leave the big dark houses of Rennie's Mill Road.

After they are married, Tom gives up masonry, goes to work at the Harvey and Brehm margarine factory, and buys a farm for his growing family on Portugal Cove Road. She runs the farm, the house, she raises three children. She spends the hours scrubbing collars that will be re-soiled with sweat.

There is a picture of Jean and Tom on the farm. It reminds me of Grant Wood's *American Gothic*, with their stern expressions and rigid pose—all it needs is a pitchfork. She glowers like a rough wind is blowing in her eyes. The face of a hard woman, or hardened.

The sea washed down our cabin,
From the berth unto the floor,
It threw me with a terrible force,
I thought that all was o'er.

In the high seas the swinging boom became a swinging weapon. And the barrels of salt, and the cargo for Bonavista, bouldering down the pitching deck. The captain's leg was broken. And the first mate's leg was broken—Jean crawled on deck to find him lying on the house.

The wounded men were got below,
And those that did not fall,
Resolved to do the best they could,
To save the lives of all.

Though she went by Jean, her siblings Tryphie and Pearce had always called her Jane. As if she was once one for nicknames. As if she once played with her sister instead of minded her, as if she once played house instead of ran one. Jane and Jean, cognates of the French Jeanne, cognate of the English John, *God is gracious.*

It was Pearce who told my grandfather about his mother's shipwreck experience. When Jean found out her brother had told, she was furious. But she kept the full story locked in her mind. She kept the poem locked in the strong box with her birth certificate and other papers, and no one knew it existed until after she had died. Her memory dressed in rhyme, like wearing a nightgown beneath the sheets for decency.

It came to me groomed by typewriter on legal paper, and photocopied many times. It is signed "Miss Jean Chaulk, Sept. 7th, 1907." But this must be the mistaken addition of whoever typed it out, for she couldn't have written it ten days before the storm.

Part of outport life is growing vegetables to stretch the fish on your plate, spreading rotting capelin on the soil. Little girls weed alongside their mothers, making chains with the piss-a-beds.

This farming in St. John's, it takes a new kind of hopefulness. Yet they can grow things here, even on this land long ago stripped of trees and blown raw. Dairy cows, hay for the dairy cows and the horses. Vegetables, chickens.

She pulls weeds in the vegetable garden—the swine cress, the wormseed, the cow vetch, the goowiddy. She picks the rocks from the land in spring, stones brought up to the surface of the soil by the winter cycle of freeze and thaw. They say that the land in Newfoundland grows rocks better than vegetables.

The thistle, the blood vine. The piss-a-beds—boil up the greens with some salt meat.

She washes the milk bottles, washes the milk bucket. Pitches the hay into the hayloft, swallowing the green musty smell.

The winters are lean. The price of fish is low and the price of vegetables is low. The world is dusty, skeletal. But they have milk and butter, eggs. Barrels in the cellar stocked with potatoes and cabbages.

She hooks mats, a new runner for the stairs. The brin stretched over the frame, sketched with pretty things. She sorts out old clothes by colour and tears them into strips. The stained housedress with the faded flowers will be worked into a new pink bloom to damp the winter drafts.

Tuesdays, the ironing.

Sometimes a knock on the door, a lean, wasting body begging for leftover vegetables, or a bit of milk.

THE DAILY NEWS, ST. JOHN'S, SEPT 21, 1907.

WORK OF STORM

Latest News.

Several messages giving further losses as a result of the storm Wednesday and Thursday, were received in town yesterday, and it is feared the end is not yet. The telegraph lines north of King's Cove are, we understand, still down, so that no reports from that part of the Island have yet been received.

SHR. DUCHESS OF FIFE

The following message was received by the Marine and Fisheries Department yesterday afternoon, from E. Button, New Melbourne: "Schooner Duchess of Fife went ashore, yesterday, at Lance Cove; total wreck; loaded with provisions for P. Templeman, Bonavista; goods practically intact. Const. Dwyer watching wreck; Captain and two of crew with legs broken; in a very precarious condition. Drs Macdonald and Pickard will do all possible for them..."

Late last night, Messrs Baine Johnstone & Co. received the following message from Mr. Barrett, of Old Perlican, "Unknown schooner lost here, points to the Effie of Trinity. Nothing human to be seen."

She raises three children but her body has born five. Ralph just six months when he died of measles. Leroy, born blue, before she even had time to teach his tiny mouth to latch. Before she had time to worry about a whoop in his cough, to watch his sputum for blood. Stillbirths and miscarriages common as a spring snow, midwives paid in fish and bread, arriving with nothing more than a bit of twine and a pair of scissors.

She is putting away the tiny sweaters, the booties, the diapers, all the clothes but the ones that will be buried. They keep her grief warm.

We drifted fast to Brownsdale,
Uncertain of our fate.
The rudder fastened with a rope,
To make her go in straight.

Edgar Pye, despite a fractured leg, spent all night at the pumps. The captain and first mate were below with broken legs in a cabin half full of water. No one was left to take control. Jean, sixteen but strong, used to seeing what needed to be done, took the wheel and steered the ship across Trinity Bay through the storm. Saving all souls on board.

Patrol Service Central Depot,
Lowestoft,
Suffolk.

10th September, 1940.

Dear Madam,

It is with very deep regret that I learn of the sad death of your son Warwick Leslie Noseworthy, Ordinary Seaman R.N.Patrol Service (H.O.), Official Number, LT/JX.208914, who is reported to have lost his life in London Docks as a result of enemy air action on 7th September, 1940.

Please allow me to express sincere sympathy with you in your bereavement on behalf of the officers and men of the Royal Navy, the high traditions of which your son has helped to maintain.

Yours sincerely,

B.H. Piercy.
COMMODORE.

Mrs. Jean Noseworthy,
Portugal Bay,
St. John's,
Newfoundland.

For some reason the letter that comes from the British Royal Navy is addressed to Jean alone, as though the death of a son in war were a particularly female burden. She sees him then, not just in dreams and faces at the other end of the street, but in silent rooms, moving as if deep in thought. Walking into the barn as if there were cows to be milked and no time for conversation.

One in the family is enough, her surviving son will be told when he tries to enlist. And for the rest of his life he will believe that it was she who somehow begged or bullied the Service Board to reject him. She will lose him anyway to the remote northern coves of Labrador, her daughter to the Canadian who whisks her away to Alberta.

And when she and Tom move into the city, her ghosts will follow her to Cavell Avenue, floating past her windows not as shapes of comfort but of loss. The way that shadows are the shape of the absence of light.

Jean immerses herself in church projects and the Women's Association, assembling care packages for soldiers, making Red Cross bandages for other mothers' sons.

When she finds her husband collapsed on the bathroom floor, she finds the muscles in her arms, built on washboards and sad irons and bread dough, the muscles and adrenaline that had heaved at the wheel when the *Duchess* pitched off Lance Cove. Enough to carry him to bed, blood in her ears like waves and the floorboards creaking beneath her staggering steps. It feels like days before the ambulance comes.

If Jean wrote him elegies, they no longer exist. She lays his body out in the parlour as the family gathers for the wake. Normally, bodies are laid out for viewing for three days before burial. But they decide to bury him after two, concerned for the state of the body poisoned with peritonitis if they wait another day.

From the N.C. Crewe File, Provincial Archives of Newfoundland:

Henry George Chaulk's daughter (Tryphena, now a widow somewhere) when returning from Labrador in a schooner, when the skipper and mate become disabled by the seas and the third man frightened, she took the wheel at Cabot Island and steered her until she ran aground in Chance Cove, Trinity Bay.

Through the years, the story has become knotted as it has passed through the hands of people on that shore. What landed in the archive is a tangle of truth and fiction. The girl, of course, was Jean Chaulk; Typhena was Jean's sister. And the ship was leaving St. John's, not Labrador. And it ran aground at Lance Cove, not Chance Cove.

The poem suggests that the same swing of the boom that broke the Captain's leg also destroyed the wheel—that the only way the ship was steered was with a rope tied to the rudder. That she couldn't have taken the wheel and steered the ship to safety. Stories here without tellers.

My mother remembers a dark and forbidden room in the house on Cavell Avenue, where little girls are not invited. She remembers a stern and bitter woman who nags her son and criticizes her daughter-in-law, a supper when her father stands up in anger and lets his plate drop down on the table, spattering gravy across the cloth. She remembers how, the night before the family is set to move to a bigger house, with room enough for the children and the new baby and a suite in the basement for Jean, Jean decides she will not move after all. How they take only their beds and leave the rest of their furniture behind for her, how she shuts herself in with her ghosts as her living son and grandchildren load their borrowed truck.

At about 2:00 in the afternoon, they sighted land. The schooner was steered aground with the hope that rescue would come from the shore. Someone made this decision, to rip the ship further apart on the faith that someone would be able to help. There must have been a violent jolt as the rocks tore into the bow of the ship. Jean would be haunted by the sound.

The Duchess *struck the reef three times,*
She then lay hard and fast
Her bottom grinding on the reef,
While seas went on her mast.

It seems that day I'll never forget,
Until my dying days.
The screaming of the women,
Amidst the winding sprays.

Perhaps she does forget. As she forgets the names of people she knew, as she forgets to turn off the stove, as she forgets the year.

Jean lives for a year by herself in the house on Cavell Avenue. She is befriended by a woman who lives across the street, who starts coming over every day. The neighbour tells Jean she is living on a dead man's pension, that Leslie went overseas to get away from her.

Dear Madam, It is with very deep regret that I learn of the sad death of your son.

Jean does not miss the armchair from the farmhouse, or the tea service she got for her wedding. Within a year, the woman has stolen almost everything Jean owns.

Perhaps she does forget that day of the wreck. Or perhaps she remembers it more clearly, the bare floorboards tilting beneath her, that grinding sound of the ship on the reef.

THE DAILY NEWS, OCT 2, 1907

Editor Daily News:

Dear Sir, — Two of the crew of the ill fated Duchess of Fife, and a passenger, a young girl of 15 or 16, arrived here yesterday, and from them we gather a sad recital of the hardships which they endured while battling for their lives...

The young lady passenger proved herself a heroine, for after the crew got broken up, she would get on deck and do all in her power for the men who were injured. Unfortunately she could not do much, as everything was soaked with water. **The name of this plucky young lady is Fanny Chalk,** and she should rank amongst the Florence Nightingales of the world...

Thanking you for space, Mr. Editor.

Yours truly,
X.Y.Z.
Brooklyn, Sept. 25th, 1907.

One day, as Jean puts out the garbage, the wind takes the storm door and takes her with it. She falls into the street and breaks her arm. The wind had been waiting all these years to break her bones.

With an arm in a cast, unable to take care of herself, Jean has no choice but to move in to my grandfather's house. And once her arm is healed, she stays, her mind continuing to erode. She accuses one of my mother's boyfriends of taking ten dollars out of her purse, another of taking her red shoes.

In the small hours of a summer night, Jean leaves the house in her nightgown and starts walking down the hill. A passing stranger stops his car and asks where she is going.

I'm going home.
Where do you live?
Cavell Avenue.

The man drives her to Cavell Avenue, and as he pulls up to the old house, he looks at her. *You're not Fraser Noseworthy's mother are you?* St. John's is still that small. *You don't live here anymore.*

My grandfather finally puts his mother in Hoyle's Home, where she is diagnosed with "senile psychosis." My mother visits her here, her stern, prim grandmother smelling like pee, with her stockings rolled down to her ankles, and stains on her blouse. The home mixes up the clothes, puts her in other women's dresses, ill-fitting on her shrunken frame. Her mouth mixes up her words, ill-fitting on her shrunken sentences. Eventually my grandfather forbids my mother to see her. Jean Chaulk Noseworthy dies in Hoyle's Home in 1975, at the age of eighty-five.

The boats were hauled both back and forth,
Till all was safe on shore.
The wounded men with fortitude,
Their suffering increased more.

The people took us to their homes,
And treated us most kind.
To tell of half they did for us,
Expressions I can't find.

Jean writes of the bravery of her fellow crewmembers, of the hospitality of the men and women who rescued them, but nothing of her own heroism. She probably never took the wheel. But there is another story, one my grandfather told, as he was told it by his uncle. As the Captain lay unconscious, the sixteen-year-old girl made a bosun chair, to lower the crew into the lifeboats sent from shore as the *Duchess* sank. She scrounged for rope and board or torn canvas, her wet fingers trembling as she rigged up the chair. She heaved the men up into her arms one by one, gently easing the Captain himself into the sling, his limp weight dragging on her shoulder.

I don't really know what a bosun chair looks like, could not find any descriptions in books on schooners or Newfoundland history, no pictures on the Internet. Hoists for window-washers on skyscrapers are also called bosun chairs. Yet I can still imagine her, slipping along the deck in pointed boots, shouting against the wind and the groan of the bow on the rocks. Soothing the men as they drop over the side of the deck. Bending against the ribs of her corset as the ship careens in the waves, somehow hoisting herself overboard. She is the last to leave the boat.

I have nothing to prove that this is true. But of all the ways to remember her, I like this one, this story.

When my grandfather was in his late seventies, he found out that his mother's name wasn't Jean. He met a distant cousin who had written a book about the area where his mother was born, who somehow knew the truth, that she was born not Jean, not Jane—nor Tryphena, nor Fanny—but Mavis. Mavis Jane Chaulk. My grandfather had his mother's birth certificate; it said her name was Jean. But in those days, it was the parishes that kept all the records of marriages, deaths, and births, and the church had burned down. When they reconstructed the records after the fire, they simply asked her what her name was.

She told them: "Jean Chaulk." And it was.

ACKNOWLEDGMENTS

I AM DEEPLY GRATEFUL to my family members who allowed me to record them, whose words have been reproduced here: Frances Bowering, Fraser Noseworthy, Nellie Noseworthy, Alice Lever, and Keith Bowering. Thanks also to those who helped me with the family research: Elizabeth Bowering and Leslie Noseworthy. I am indebted to my great-grandparents, John Bowering and Jean Chaulk, whose poems "Trip of the Ill-Fated *Swallow*" and "The Loss of the *Duchess of Fife*" I have quoted.

Thanks to the many writers and friends who provided feedback on various stages of this book. Particular thanks to Ted Bishop for his mentorship in the early stages of this project, to the writers of A Drift Collective, and to my editor, Jenna Butler.

Different versions of sections of this book have been published in *Geist* 91 (2014) and *Prairie Fire* 25.1 (2004). I am grateful to their skilled editors. Thanks in particular to AnnMarie MacKinnon for her patient and generous work on "The Bosun Chair."

In researching this book I consulted many resources, including Newfoundland and Labrador Heritage, *Cows Don't Know it's Sunday: Agricultural Life in St. John's* by Hilda Chaulk Murray; *More than 50%: A Woman's Life in a Newfoundland Outport, 1900-1950*, by Hilda Chaulk Murray; *As Near to Heaven By Sea*, by Kevin Major; and *The Dictionary of Newfoundland English*, edited by G.M. Story, W.J. Kirwin, and J.D.A. Widdowson.

Portions of articles have been reproduced from the *St. John's Daily News* and the *Bay Roberts Guardian*. Photos used throughout the book have come from family collections.

JENNIFER BOWERING DELISLE was born in Edmonton, AB, and has published poetry, fiction and non-fiction in a variety of literary magazines. She completed a PhD in English in 2008 at the University of British Columbia and has held postdoctoral fellowships at the University of Alberta and McMaster University. She is the author of *The Newfoundland Diaspora: Mapping the Literature of Out-Migration* (Wilfrid Laurier University Press, 2013). She currently resides in Edmonton, Alberta.